MAYAN
Legends

Contents

Introduction

Whenever you hear speak of Yucatan, you have to remember that this place possesses a past rich in history and traditions. Here the yesteryear of wondrous cities at Chichén Itzá, Uxmal, Tulum, Cobá, Edzná, and other pre-Hispanic sites blends with the heritage of the Conquistadores to form a religious syncretism which — when added to fearful superstitions toward beings cloaked in magic and mystery — has produced the myths and legends of this marvelous land: the Mayab, "land of the chosen".

Preserved in the sacred books of the Maya like the Popol Vuh and the Chilam Balam, and influenced by European legends and beliefs, the myths of Yucatan have provided a way of explaining and justifying natural phenomena, illness and even what we call "fate", as well as transmitting positive human values.

But this legacy would not have reached us if it had not been for the oral tradition. This is one of the most important characteristics of the indigenous cultures of America, and it has thus kept the soul of Yucatan alive and thriving in the towns and villages of the region.

Editorial Dante now presents the most important characters who people the legends of Yucatan: the stormy love affairs of the X' Tabay, perhaps the best-known character in the folklore of the Peninsula; the dark powers of the Huay Chivo; the desperation of Nicte Ha; the daring of the Dwarf of Uxmal; the misfortune of the Maquech; and the beneficence and wisdom of Itzamná. Our aim is for you the reader of these stories to come closer to and understand another aspect of the rich cultural heritage which the Mayan world has to offer.

The X' Tabay

Suluay was a young girl who lived in a small village in Yucatan, at the time when Chichén Itzá was in its greatest splendor.

Every evening the lovely maiden would sit at the entrance to her house and comb her long, jet-black hair with leaves from the breadnut tree. And there was no man who was not captivated, at least a little, by that lithe figure and those eyes that recalled the warm summer nights of the Mayab.

Among these men was the son of the village chief, a young warrior who fell deeply and sincerely in love with the young girl, and asked for her hand in marriage.

Suluay was equally enamored of the handsome young heir, and accepted joyfully.

However, this union was not to everyone's liking. A young sorceress who lived on the edge of the village had also fallen for the chief's son, but had been re-jected. She was most grieved by the pair of lovers, and hatched a plan to tear them apart.

Using her knowledge of dark magic, she went into the depths of the forest to seek out the roots and herbs that would help her separate the couple. She mixed them into a brew which she added to a jug of corn milk.

In order to get close to her victim, the witch pretended she wanted to congratulate the young girl on her upcoming wedding. Suluay, unaware that drinking the corn milk would be her downfall, thanked the witch for the gift and drained it to the last drop.

That night, Suluay began to experience emotions she had never felt before. Little by little, her flesh and blood were overwhelmed by uncontrollable desire. Prey to her irresistible passions, she went out into the village eagerly determined to satisfy them.

However, rather than slaking her desire, she found that her appetite grew ever fiercer. In the morning the whole village knew that Suluay had succumbed to the pleasures of the flesh in the arms of every man there.

Of course, word reached the ears of the chief's son. Consumed by anger and jealousy, he sought out Suluay to demand an explanation for her behavior. The

girl could only dimly remember what had happened, and was unable to explain herself. The anguished warrior decided to end the engage-

ment, and then went to a nearby kapok tree and hanged himself from its branches.

When she heard what had happened, Suluay immediately took her own life as well, cursing all the men who had been the cause of her misery.

From that time on, it is a well-known fact that behind every kapok tree one may come across a woman combing her long, jet-black tresses, as she waits in hiding to call any passing man who might want to satisfy his lust. But later he will pay with his life, dying amid fevered hallucinations in atonement for those who caused her to lose her happiness forever.

Maquech

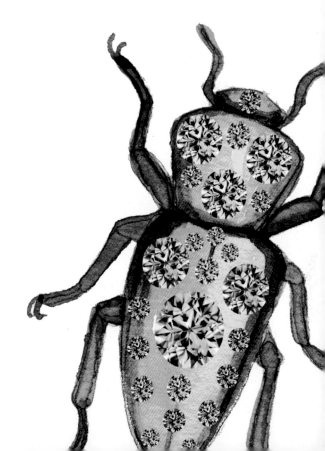

Cuzam was a beautiful Mayan princess, the daughter of a powerful king, in the days when the cities of the Mayab shone like gold.

This king loved his daughter dearly, and she had no whim that was not satisfied. For her part, the princess was a model of obedience and virtue.

When Cuzam became old enough to marry, her father betrothed her to Nan Chan, son of another great monarch from a neighboring kingdom.

Nan Chan was a good, respectful man, and so the young girl was happy to accept the arrangement.

But one day, while she was in the great hall of the palace, receiving the trophies of war which her father sent her after every battle, Cuzam met a handsome young warrior named Chacpol.

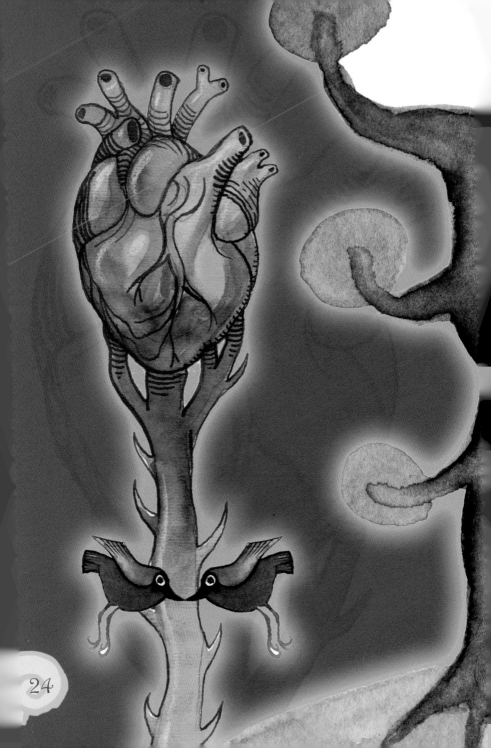

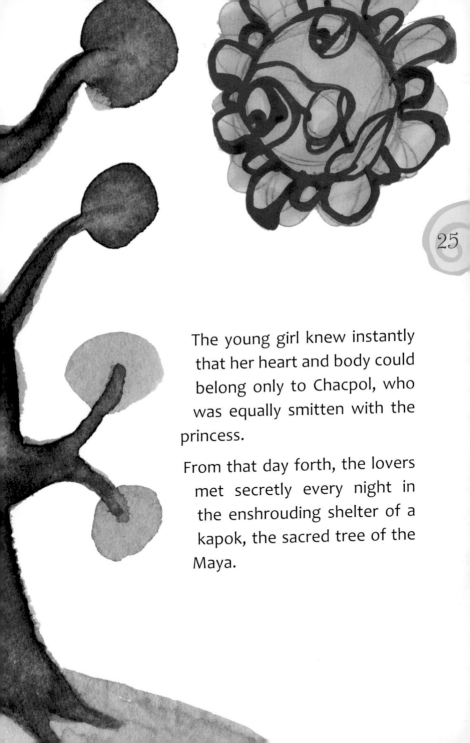

The young girl knew instantly that her heart and body could belong only to Chacpol, who was equally smitten with the princess.

From that day forth, the lovers met secretly every night in the enshrouding shelter of a kapok, the sacred tree of the Maya.

But their true happiness was fleeting: eventually word of their clandestine relationship reached the ears of the Cuzam's father. In his rage, he ordered the warrior sacrificed. No matter how hard the girl begged for the life of her lover, the king would not bend, and commanded that the young man should die.

On the day of the sacrifice, the princess again begged her father for the life of Chacpol, promising

that if it were saved, she would in return marry her betrothed Nan Chan.

The king consulted the priests, who agreed to spare the warrior.

That night, Cuzam was summoned before the *Halach Uinic*. The king was there with a sorcerer, who came to Cuzam and gave her a beetle. "This is Chacpol," he said. "Though your father released him from the sacrifice, he ordered him transformed for having dared to love you".

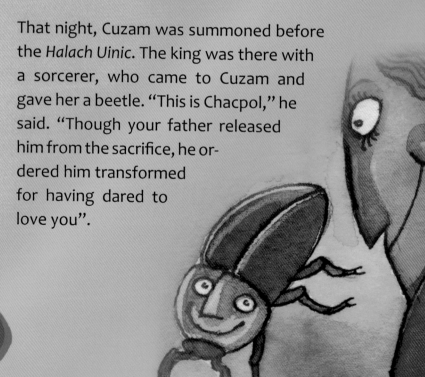

The princess was sad but resigned. She took the insect tenderly, and had it covered in the finest precious stones in the kingdom and fastened to it a chain of purest gold.

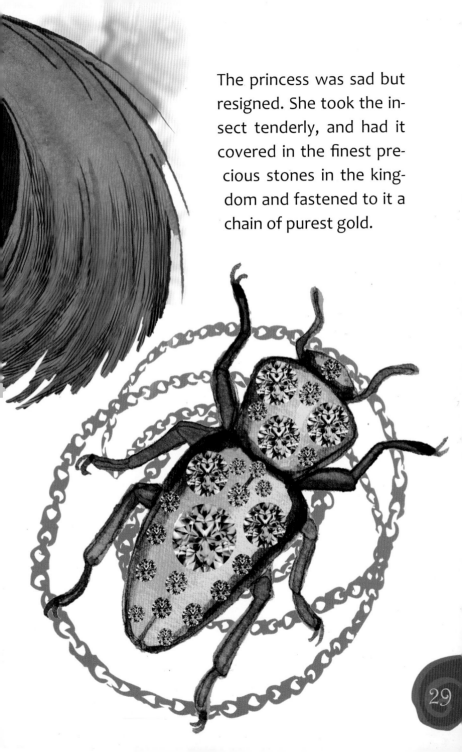

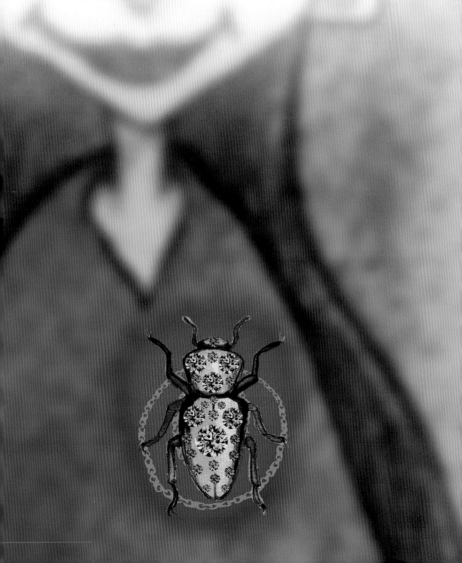

Then she placed it on her breast, saying. "I shall marry another man, but I shall never part from you... you shall forever hear the beating of my heart, where you shall live eternally".

And so it was.

The Dwarf of Uxmal

They say that in a village of the Mayab called Nohpat, there lived a sorceress who understood the mysteries of the skies and knew the properties of roots and herbs, and how to use them to cure any ill.

When she was well advanced in age, the woman desired to

have a son, so she went to a secret place from where she brought back an egg, which she incubated. From it was born a boy, and when he spoke, everyone was amazed by his wisdom. As the years passed he grew up, but not in stature, remaining no more than seven hands in height.

He was intelligent enough to notice that his grand-mother never moved far from the three hearth-stones in her house, and he wondered what was hidden there. One day, when the old woman was distracted, he quickly reached into the ashes and found a *tunkul*, a wooden drum, which he struck with a stick.

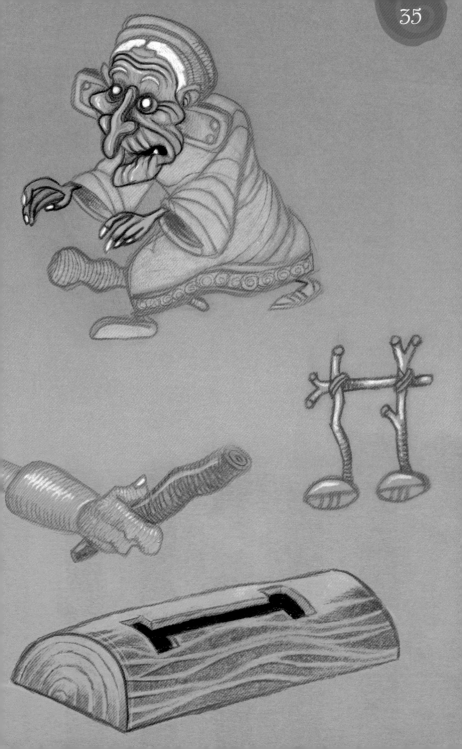

He beat the drum so hard that the sound was heard far and wide. The sorceress returned, very angry, and told him that what he had done would change destiny, and that terrible events would occur, in which he would find himself embroiled.

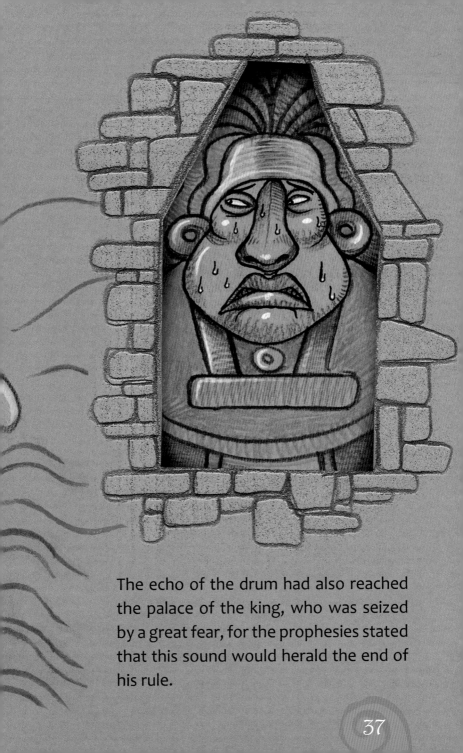

The echo of the drum had also reached the palace of the king, who was seized by a great fear, for the prophesies stated that this sound would herald the end of his rule.

However, his counselors advised him to seek out the person who had played the *tunkul* to see if it really was the one who would succeed him on the throne.

In their search, the king's guards came to Nohpat, where they found the dwarf and took him to the palace.

When the dwarf was brought before him, the king asked if he really was who he claimed to be, and if so, to prove it by showing the wisdom that any ruler must possess.

After the dwarf had answered several questions very astutely, the king decided upon a final test: this would consist in breaking a *cocoyol* nut with a hammer on the head of the dwarf. The dwarf agreed, on condition that the king would then undergo the same test.

42

The royal executioner placed the *cocoyol* on the dwarf's head and struck it hard, but the dwarf arose, smiling. When the king submitted to the test, he was killed instantly. The dwarf survived because the sorceress had hidden a cap of enchanted copper under his hair.

So the dwarf was proclaimed king of Uxmal. That very day his grandmother called him and told him that she would not live much longer, but that now that he was king, she could die in peace.

44 "Act with justice, and always face the truth," the old woman told him. "Do not forget it is more important to be good than to be just. Listen to the voice of the gods and follow their counsel, but listen also to the voice of men. Never despise the lowly, and distrust the powerful."

For many years, the dwarf followed his grandmother's advice, and peace and harmony reigned at Uxmal. But with the passing of time the dwarf began to abuse his authority: he became tyrannical, vain and cruel.

The gods were offended by this behavior, and punished the city. Thousands of warriors fell upon it, sacked it and burned it, erasing forever the memory of its people and of the dwarf who had once reigned over them.

The Goat-Wizard Huay Chivo

They say that not long after the Conquest there
lived on the outskirts of a village in the east of
Yucatan a man who took pleasure in magical arts.
He understood the secrets of plants, he knew what
prayers would cure sickness, and which would cause
it, and since he was a child he had been able to control the animals of field and forest.

They also say that this sorcerer had a black heart, filled with bitterness because of his unrequited love for a beautiful young girl: worse yet, she did everything she could to avoid him whenever he tried to approach her, because of the stories told about him, but above all, because she was afraid of him.

The girl lived with her parents, aging countryfolk whom she helped by looking after the animals on their plot of land. Her favorites were the goats, and she spent most of her time with them, finding refuge there in times of joy and moments of sadness.

One day, after he had pressed his suit insistently to the young girl, and fired with uncontrollable passion, the wizard invoked the powers of darkness to help him be with the woman who rejected him. His entreaties were heard, but in return he would have to give up half his soul to the lords of the underworld, and the other half could remain only in the form of a beast.

He chose the form of a goat, since he knew the peasant girl loved them.

From that moment on, every time that the passion for his beloved arose, the sorcerer would utter prayers and undergo strange contortions to become half man and half goat so that he could be close to her, albeit only in this form.

Even today, in some parts of Yucatan, they say that this creature can be seen at night, perhaps searching among the women for the one who could never love him.

The Discovery of henequén

The Itzaes, a brave and peaceful group of Maya have been in these lands since time immemorial.

They were led by a priest named Zamná, and while

they were resting after their arduous journey, he recalled the words spoken to him by the queen of Atlantis:

"Our land will disappear within one moon. Since you are the wisest and best of my people, I have chosen you as guide and messenger of my commands.

Choose a group of families and three *chilames*. You shall go to a place which I will show you, and there you will found a city. You will build a high temple and beneath it you will keep the texts that recount our history, and those that will be written in the future.

You and the chosen ones shall sail to the west in nine ships. After nine days you will find an uninhabited land with rivers and mountains, and there you will enter. You will wait until you find water, and there you shall found the city as I have commanded you."

On the second day of sailing after they had set off, a storm sank two of the boats. Zamná thought that the end had come for the group, but the storm waned.

Finally they came to the uninhabited land of rivers and mountains foretold by the queen, but there was no water: the land was dry, and covered in a strange plant, very green, with hard, sharp, pointed leaves.

Suddenly the sky became dark and heavy rain began to fall. The travelers were happy to receive this water from heaven, but they did not know how long it would last, so Zamná arranged for some of it to be stored.

As he passed by one of the strange plants, a thorn speared his foot. When the Itzaes saw this, they punished the plant by cutting off the leaf and beating it violently against the stones of the place.

However, Zamná noticed that the leaves produced a tough fiber that could be useful for the people. He realized that his wound had been a sign, and ordered them to stop punishing the plant.

Meanwhile, the rain continued, and the water flowed through a gap in the rocks. Zamná followed the stream and discovered the place indicated by the queen.

So then the priest joined the vitality of the water, the power of heaven, the essence of the chosen ones and the strength of the plant — which he named *henequén* — and he founded the great city we now know as Izamal.

The Story of Nicte Ha

Chacdziedzib was a Prince of the Mayab in days of legend, and among his people he was venerated as just and brave, as well as an expert shot with the bow.

He was deeply in love with Nicte Ha, the daughter of the guardian of the Sacred Cenote. Every night they met nearby to express their love, and only parted when the rays of the sun began to part the shadows.

This relationship was not to the liking of many, because Nicte Ha was not a princess. One day the priests of the place decided that the affair had to end, since it was necessary — for the good of the kingdom — that Chacdziedzib marry a princess from

another city. So they resolved that Nicte Ha should be sacrificed. Their plan was overheard by someone close to the young prince, who immediately sent a warrior to fetch Nicte Ha so that he could take her formally for his wife.

But the warrior could not carry out the prince's errand, because he was mysteriously murdered before he could find the girl.

When he found out, the prince took his bow and went to the sacred Cenote in search of his beloved. He found her there, but from the deep shadows an arrow sped straight to Nicte Ha's heart, and she fell lifeless into the Cenote.

Chacdziedzib watched helplessly as she disappeared beneath the sacred waters, leaving only her dress floating on the surface. Filled with grief, the young

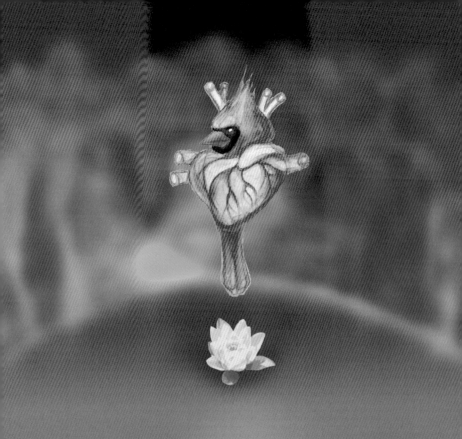

man sank to his knees on the blood of his love and prayed to the gods for mercy.

The gods heard his entreaty and took pity on him, transforming Nicte Ha into a water lily, and Chacdziedzib's own heart into a beautiful red bird called a cardinal.

And today, at dawn in the cenotes of Yucatan, you can still see this bird perching on the leaves of its beloved flower...

MAYAN Legends
1st Edition, 1st reprint, June 2012

I.S.B.N. 978-607-7857-07-5

D.R. © Editorial Dante S.A. de C.V.
Calle 17 No. 138-B esq. Prol. Paseo de Montejo
Col. Itzimná, C.P. 97100, Mérida, Yucatán, México.

Editor in chief: Hervé Baeza Braga
Creative control: Gabriela Calero Cervera
Graphic design: Gabriela Calero Cervera
Texts: Svetlana Larrocha
Illustrations: Tony Peraza (cartonysta@hotmail.com)
Translation: David Phillips
Copy checking: Laura Morales Encalada

PRINTED IN CHINA